W9-AYW-048

Skip to My Lou

Repeat the melody for each verse in the song.

Chorus

Lou, Lou, skip to my Lou, Lou, Lou, skip to my Lou,

Lou, Lou, skip to my Lou, Skip to my Lou, my dar - ling!

To my mother and father

Copyright © 1989 by Nadine Bernard Westcott
Series Editor, Mary Ann Hoberman
More fun with Skip to My Lou! activity page © 2003 by Little, Brown and Company (Inc.)

All rights reserved. No part of this book may be reproduced in any form or by
any electronic or mechanical means, including information storage and retrieval
systems, without permission in writing from the publisher, except by a reviewer
who may quote brief passages in a review.

First Edition

The Sing-Along Stories logo design is a trademark of Little, Brown and Company (Inc.).

Library of Congress Cataloging-in-Publication Data
Westcott, Nadine Bernard.
    Skip to my Loud / by Nadine Bernard Westcott. — 1st ed.
        p. cm.
    Summary: When his parents leave a young boy in charge of the farm for a day, chaos erupts as
the animals take over the house.
    ISBN 0-316-73406-3 (hc)
    ISBN 0-316-93140-3 (pb)
    [1. Farm life — Fiction. 2. Humorous stories. 3. Stories in rhyme.] I. Title.

PZ8.3.W4998Sk   1989
[E]—dc219   88-7306

10 9 8 7 6 5 4 3 2

SC

Manufactured in China

The illustrations for this book were done in watercolor and ink.
The text was set in Korinna, and the display type is Fontoon.

Skip to My Lou

Adapted and illustrated by Nadine Bernard Westcott

Series Editor, Mary Ann Hoberman

Megan Tingley Books
LITTLE, BROWN AND COMPANY
New York · An AOL Time Warner Company

Sitting on the front porch,
Painted like new —
The farm's all in order,
There's not much to do.

"Take care of the farm.
We'll be back by two!"

Skip to my Lou, my darling!

Flies in the sugarbowl,

Shoo fly shoo.

Cats in the buttermilk,

Two by two.

Pigs in the parlor,
What'll I do?

Skip to my Lou, my darling!

Cows in the kitchen,
Moo cow moo.

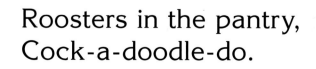

Roosters in the pantry,
Cock-a-doodle-do.

Sheep in the bathtub,
Hulla-baloo!

Skip to my Lou, my darling!

Lou, Lou, skip to my Lou,

Lou, Lou, skip to my Lou,
Lou, Lou, skip to my Lou,
Skip to my Lou, my darling!

Look at the clock,
It's a quarter to two!
Goodness gracious,
What will we do?

Hurry, quick! It's up to you!

Skip to my Lou, my darling!

Phew!

More fun with *Skip to My Lou!*

❶ Look at the first picture in this book. Since the farm is all in order, the little boy in the picture doesn't have much to do. Think of the many different things to do on a farm. Draw a picture of the little boy doing one of those things.

❷ The farmer and his wife are expected to return at two o'clock, so the little boy and the animals begin getting the farm back in order at a quarter to two. Draw a clock that shows two o'clock (2:00) and another clock that shows a quarter to two (1:45). Which hands point to the hour? Which point to the minutes? Try to guess what time the little boy wakes up and goes to bed. Draw a clock that shows these times.

❸ Look at the page without words where the little boy and the animals are cleaning up the farm. Make up a verse to go with each picture (for example, "Cow sweeps, moo cow moo.").

❹ Count the words in the song that rhyme with "Lou" and "two." Can you think of other words that rhyme with "Lou"?

❺ Sing the song and skip to the rhythm. Then clap to the rhythm. Perform the song using rhythm instruments, such as tambourines, drumsticks, and shakers.

Activities prepared by Pat Scales, Director of Library Services, South Carolina Governor's School for the Arts and Humanities, Greenville, SC.